HOW TO LIVE LIKE

AN AZTEC PRIEST

Thanks to the creative team:
Senior Editor: Alice Peebles
Consultant: John Haywood
Fact checking: Kate Mitchell
Design: www.collaborate.agency

Hungry Tomato™
A division of Lerner Publishing Group, Inc.
241 First Avenue North
Minneapolis, MN 55401 USA

For reading levels and more information,
look up this title at www.lernerbooks.com.

Main body text set in Century Gothic Regular 10/13.
Typeface provided by Monotype Typography.

Library of Congress Cataloging-in-Publication Data

Library of Congress Cataloging-in-Publication Data

Names: Farndon, John, author. | Aloisi, Giuliano, illustrator.
Title: How to live like an Aztec priest / by John Farndon ;
illustrator: Giuliano Aloisi.
Description: Minneapolis : Hungry Tomato, 2016. | Series: How to live like... |
Includes index. | Audience: Ages 8-12. | Audience: Grades 4 to 6.
Identifiers: LCCN 2015048780 (print) | LCCN 2016004578 (ebook) |
ISBN 9781512406283 (lb : alk. paper) | ISBN 9781512411652 (pb : alk. paper)
| ISBN 9781512409154 (eb pdf)
Subjects: LCSH: Aztecs—Juvenile literature. | Aztecs—Social life and
customs—Juvenile literature.
Classification: LCC F1219.73 .F37 2016 (print) | LCC F1219.73 (ebook) |
DDC 972/.01—dc23

LC record available at http://lccn.loc.gov/2015048780

Manufactured in the United States of America
1 – VP – 7/15/16

HOW TO LIVE LIKE
AN AZTEC
PRIEST

by John Farndon
Illustrated by Giuliano Aloisi

HUNGRY
TOMATO.

contents

Building an Empire

It's the year 1518 and you're in the middle of the Aztec Empire. I'm called Ten Vulture because I was born on the tenth day of the Vulture month. This is where I grew up—Xochimilco. It looks peaceful, doesn't it? Just small *chinampas* (fields) of corn watered by cool, tree-lined canals. But don't let the quiet fool you! We Aztecs won this area by being harder and bloodier than anyone else. Our warriors are tough and super-scary. But our soldiers are rabbits compared to our priests—and I'm going to become one. So you'd better watch out!

The Aztec Empire

Nobody knows where our people, the Mexica, came from. But we arrived here two centuries ago. The local king drove us from the land after we killed his daughter as a sacrifice, so we built our city Tenochtitlan in Lake Texcoco. Then, sixty years ago, we formed an alliance with other kings to create a great empire, with our city at its heart. Aztecs rule, ok?

Tuxpan

Tenochtitlan

Gulf of Mexico

Aztec Empire

Huaxyacac

North Pacific Ocean

We had no dry land, so we built islands in the lake to grow our crops. These are the chinampas shown here. We make a square fence with twigs in the lake. Then we fill in the middle with mud from the lake bed and rotting vegetation to make soil.

Our empire depends on war. We need wars to capture people to sacrifice in the temples and repay the gods. Every man must fight in the army, and every commander must prove himself by capturing people to sacrifice.

The Mighty Gods

We Aztecs have many gods, and we are in awe of them. They are powerful and we must show our thanks to them at all times for making the world, or they will bring catastrophe to us. So we build many temples to worship them, and sacrifice to them the greatest gift we can give—human life. We must suffer pain, too, as we believe the gods suffered to give us life. The mighty god Huitzilopochtli is the sun and fights the forces of night to keep us alive. He must have blood every day to give him strength for the fight, allowing the sun to rise next day!

It is an honor to be an *ixiptla*—a person chosen to dress up as a god, and who is later killed for the god.

Coatlicue: mother of gods

Huitzilopochtli: Hummingbird of the South, a ferocious warrior god armed with a fire snake

Itztlacoliuhqui: god of ice and cold, armed with a sharp obsidian blade

Mictlantecuhtli: god of the dead, a skeleton with bloody spots

Quetzalcoatl: the feathered serpent god of wind and wisdom

Tezcatlipoca: the smoking mirror, god of the night sky and memory

Tlaloc: god of storms

Xipe Totec: god of flayed skins, harvest, and rebirth

Xolotl: god of fire, sickness, and deformity

Xochiquetzal: goddess of beauty

Will You Be a Priest?

My fate was decided when I was just a baby. My dad and mom wanted me to be a priest. So they invited the great old men, the *quaquacuiltin*, of the *calmecac* training school to a great banquet to offer me to them. Luckily, the wise men agreed and they took me off to the calmecac at once! There they painted me entirely black and hung a string of wooden beads called *tlacopotli* around my neck. The beads took on my soul. So my soul was kept at the school in the beads, and I was sent back to my dad and mom for the next fifteen years, until I was ready to train.

You're in Hot Chilies, Son!

As you grow up, you are taught that life is painful and dangerous. You must fetch water, gather firewood, and fish for food. You must learn to be honest and quiet. If you're not, once you are seven years old, you will be punished to repay your debt to the gods. You might be held over a fire of roasting chilies, so the smoke stings your eyes, nose, and throat.

Our moms and dads believe children only grow if they are stretched frequently. So they regularly pull our hands, fingers, arms, legs, feet, neck, noses, and ears to make us grow. It's especially important to stretch us if there's an earthquake.

To calmecac

I am fifteen years old, and it's my first day at the calmecac. It is a really big day. I will not see my family again for a long, long time. Dad leaves me at the entrance to the school and I wave goodbye. I will not cry. I have already learned to be tough. Calmecac means "House of Being Sorry"— so you know it won't all be fun! The calmecac that I am attending is right inside the temple complex in Tenochtitlan. So every day I see the great steps up the pyramid where I will surely walk one day.

Making Music

Learning music is great! We sing and we bang on the *teponaztli* drum made from a log, rattle the *yoyotl*, and blow on flutes. But music is also serious. Musical instruments are sacred, and we learn to play music for religious ceremonies. We beat drums as we observe the stars at night and sound conch shell trumpets as we make sacrifices.

Some Aztec boys go to the *telpochcalli* school. There they train to become soldiers, not priests. The training is intense, and this is what makes our army so invincible.

13

Hard Schooling

School is so, so tough! When we finish lessons, we sweep floors, dig fields, gather firewood, and cook. And at midnight we are woken up to pray… and jump into an icy pool! We also suffer the Staying Awake at Night ritual, which means not sleeping for five days or more. In lessons, we learn our people's songs and history. We learn about astronomy and the calendar. We learn how to interpret dreams and omens from the gods. And we learn how to fight.

Getting the Point!

There's no slacking at this school, I can tell you. Sometimes I'm so tired. But if priests catch you nodding off, even for a second, they punish you. You must learn to suffer. They jab you with maguey cactus spikes. Sometimes, they send you out into the desert in the middle of the night—and you have to jab yourself!

Those of us who are to be priests also learn a special language. And I'm learning how to make things from bird feathers, since I want to follow Quetzalcoatl, the feathered serpent god.

We learn some of our lessons from books. They're written mostly on paper made from tree bark and they fold into pleats like an accordian. The writing is in painted pictures, not words. The Spanish later called this kind of book a *codex*.

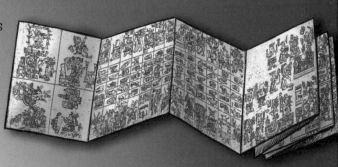

The Great city

Our school is at the very heart of Tenochtitlan, right next to the great temples. More than two hundred thousand people live in Tenochtitlan, and it takes almost an hour to walk across the city! Yet it is right in the middle of a lake, on islands created by our people a century ago. Whenever I get a spare moment from school, I go and explore. Just outside the temple complex walls is the *tecpan*, the new palace of our great emperor Moctezuma II. Right next to that is the great square where they hold the market. On the other side of the square is the old palace of Axayacatl.

The big market between the palaces is the most exciting place in the city. It's so noisy and full of color! If you have money—cacao beans, which serve as our money—you can get anything imaginable here! Do you want a quail for dinner, or an eagle? No problem. Or how about some chocolate? Do you need a new shirt? What color? How about gold? You can buy bird quills stuffed with gold powder. And officials go around making sure you don't get ripped off.

View of Tenochtitlan

Here's a view of Tenochtitlan, On the left, you can see the great pyramid in the temple complex. My school is at the foot of the temple, on the left. To the right of the temples is the great square where they hold the biggest market, with the royal palaces on either side. Tenochtitlan, with its cool canals and green gardens, is so beautiful. One of our poets wrote, "The city spreads in rings of jade, its spokes flashing light like quetzal [feathers], Here [along the canals] lords are borne in boats, bathed in a flowery mist."

Playing Ball

One day we had a day off school, and some of us went to the ball game called *tlachtli*. It's really exciting—and dangerous. It's played in a large stone court, and two teams battle it out to knock a rubber ball through a ring high on the court wall. You can't use your hands or feet to hit the ball, only hips, knees, legs, and elbows. But there are no rules to stop you from hitting your opponents. That's why players often get badly hurt! But my team just won! Yes!!!

Spinning

The most dangerous game of all is *volador*. It's played as a tribute to the gods. Young men dress up as birds to jump from a very high pole with a rope tied around their waist. They spin through the air thirteen times. With luck, they unroll to land on their feet just before they hit the ground. But they're not always lucky!

Stories go around that the losing team gets killed. That's just an old story. But it is true that the winning team in a big match is allowed to take things from those watching—including their clothes!

Board Game

Patolli is a man's game and if we're caught playing it, we're in trouble! You throw five beans, each with a marked and a plain side, to race pieces around the board. You bet on who'll get his pieces off the board first.

off to war

Even we priests learn to fight. And now we are going to war for real! I'm scared but excited. I've been awake all night, shivering! Now it's dawn, and columns of smoke tell us the battle will soon begin. Suddenly, the silence is broken by the boom of drums and the roar of trumpets. At once, the foot soldiers launch a deadly volley of arrows from bows and stones from slings. Then the Shorn Ones, the elite shaven-headed warriors, charge against the enemy, followed by the Eagle and Jaguar warriors. Boys in their first battle, like me, follow in the rear. Here we go!!

I took captives for sacrifice! So now I can cut my hair and wear a full-length, white *tlahuiztli* (war suit), the mark of the goddess Tlazolteotl. If that other coward hadn't got away, I'd have earned a green *tlahuiztli* and the feathers of Quetzalcoatl. Four captives gets you a red suit!

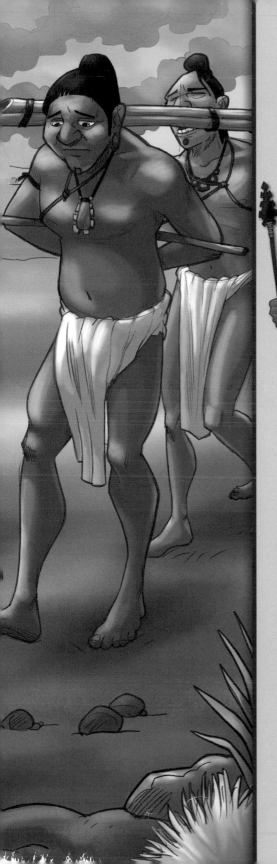

Eagles and Jaguars

Only a few become Shorn Ones, sworn never to turn back in battle. But all young warriors want to capture enough prisoners to become one of the elite Eagles or Jaguars.

Eagle Warrior

You can easily tell an Eagle in battle, because he wears an eagle's head helmet, and covers his body in feathers. After a battle, the Eagles are allowed to eat in the royal palace and drink *pulque* (beer). You must have done twenty great deeds to become an Eagle.

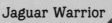

Jaguar Warrior

These warriors dress as the fiercest animal in our land. Aztecs believe the costume gives them the big cat's strength. To become a Jaguar, you have to capture twelve enemies in one battle, and twelve in the next.

Becoming a Little Priest

I've finally finished at the calmecac, but my training as a priest is only just beginning. I'm now living in the temple of Quetzalcoatl itself! I am an apprentice priest or *Tlamacazton* (little priest). And I am learning all the holiest secret rituals from a *Tlamacazqui*—a priest of offerings. We may only speak to each other in the secret language of the priesthood, and I still don't speak it well. So, it's hard for me. And we must often fast (not eat) and prick ourselves with spikes to show our dedication.

I am at the very lowest level of priests in the temple. Above me are many different priests. Above the Tlamacazqui are the *Tlenamacac* priests. And above them there are so many different kinds of priests that I forget them all. I remember Ometochtizn, the priest of beer and singing!

These are some of my tasks for the day!

1 Keep track of the time.

2 Update the calendar.

3 Record events in picture words.

4 Keep track of the moon and stars, and look for eclipses.

5 Study horoscopes to make the right chants to the gods.

6 Study horoscopes for the people.

7 Select and make offerings and sacrifices to the gods.

8 Perform rites to keep the gods from bringing disaster on us.

9 Hear confessions.

10 Train boys who will become priests with night walks to collect dangerous creatures, so they learn to face death.

Entering the Great Temple

Today I am going up the great temple mound, the *huei teocalli*. It marks the spot where the god Huitzilopochtli told our people they had reached their new home. At its foot there is a rack holding bloody heads from the latest sacrifices. *Uugh!* I shudder and follow the priest up the steps. It is 200 feet (60 meters) to the top, and the view far over the city makes you gasp. In the middle of the vast platform are two temples, dedicated to the gods of our two greatest needs: Huitzilopochtli for war and Tialoc for farming.

The temple mound is a symbol for the hill of Coatepec. Here the god Huitzilopochtli was born. His sister planned to kill him, but he cut off her head and laid it at the foot of the mound. That is why the skull racks are there.

The Hummingbird

Huitzilpochtli's name means "the hummingbird," but he is the god of war. We depend on him for all our victories in war. That's why we must sustain him with new sacrifices all the time.

sacrifice

Our great task is to sacrifice to the gods. Soldiers go to war so they can bring back men, women, and children to be killed. Then we can show our thanks to the gods, for we must return their gift of life. Today, I have painted my face black and my body red, and I will stand on top of the temple with the high priest. Soldiers will lead the sacrifices up the steps to us and we will throw each one across the altar. The high priest will plunge in the stone knife, slice out the heart, and hold it up to the gods in offering. The steps turn red with blood.

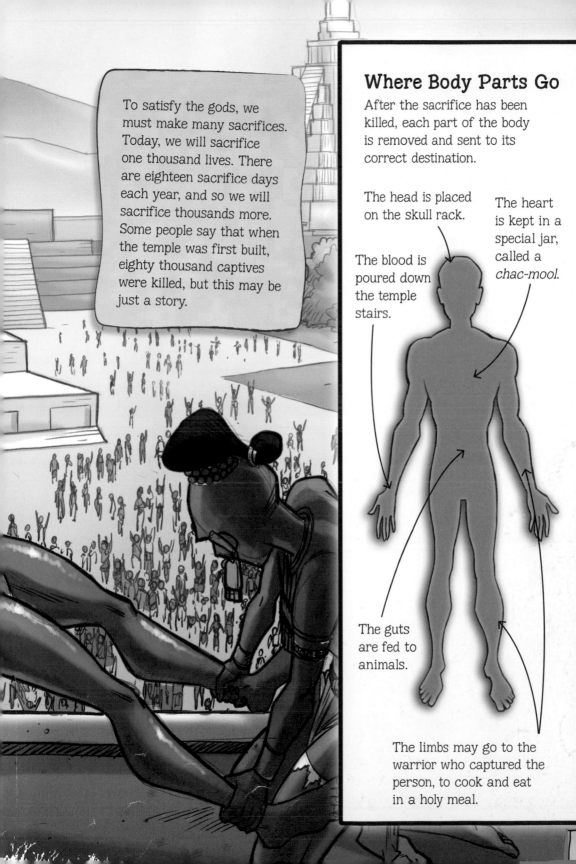

To satisfy the gods, we must make many sacrifices. Today, we will sacrifice one thousand lives. There are eighteen sacrifice days each year, and so we will sacrifice thousands more. Some people say that when the temple was first built, eighty thousand captives were killed, but this may be just a story.

Where Body Parts Go

After the sacrifice has been killed, each part of the body is removed and sent to its correct destination.

The head is placed on the skull rack.

The heart is kept in a special jar, called a *chac-mool*.

The blood is poured down the temple stairs.

The guts are fed to animals.

The limbs may go to the warrior who captured the person, to cook and eat in a holy meal.

Making It to the Top

I have made great progress through the priesthood. I have been dedicated and determined. I have proved myself again and again by spiking myself and denying myself rest. And I have helped with many sacrifices. I have become a fire priest or *tlenamacac*. It is the greatest honor that a priest can have. It means I can use the great knife of sacrifice myself. And I am one of the chosen few who may stand at the right hand of Moctezuma II, the emperor—or Great Speaker, as we call him—who is half a god.

Moctezuma II was our last ruler! In 1519, just a year after I stood by him in my glory, the Spanish soldiers came. They killed Moctezema and destroyed Tenochtitlan and our entire way of life.

Our people are divided into different levels, and each of us has his or her level. At the top are the *tlatoani* (rulers); then come important warriors, priests, and priestesses; next there are lords—while other warriors are found at all ranks of society; then there are *pochteca* (merchants and craftspeople); and at the bottom are *macehualli* (peasants, slaves, and servants).

Rulers: Great Speaker or King

Priests, Priestesses, and Eagle and Jaguar warriors

Lords

Merchants and Craftspeople →

Peasants, → Slaves, and Servants

Butterflies and Birds

When soldiers die in battle, we believe their souls will in time become butterflies or hummingbirds. When merchants are killed on a trading mission, their souls also become butterflies or hummingbirds. Ordinary people become flowers, or go to the underworld to serve the Lord of the Land of the Dead, Mictlanteuctl.

Ten Awesome Aztec Facts

1 Every fifty-two years or so, at the New Fire Festival, everyone put out their fires for five days, until a fire had been lit in the chest of a sacrifice victim. Then they relit their fires and partied for twelve days!

2 Aztecs believed that the sun they lived under was the fifth sun. When it ended, the world would be destroyed by an earthquake.

3 They also believed everything, from life to the heavens, came from the cut-up pieces of the gods' bodies. That was why they made sacrifices: to repay their debt to the gods.

4 To repay their debt to the god Quetzalcoatl, the Aztecs sacrificed butterflies and hummingbirds to him.

5 No one could look at the emperor's face or turn their back on him. So the Aztecs had to face him with their heads always bowed low. Lords had to take off their shoes and wear only a sack when they visited.

6 Girls made spit beer from balls of corn they chewed and spat out. It was considered delicious!

7 Boys who were destined for the priesthood were scarred on the chest and hips with the spine of a stringray. Boys who were to be soldiers had their lips pierced.

8 Priests never washed or cut their hair, so it became matted and stinky.

9 The month of Ochpaniztli (September) was the cleaning month. Ordinary people went out and swept the streets spotlessly clean, then jumped in the river for a good wash!

10 One of their favorite foods was cakes made from the green scum (an algae called spirulina) on ponds. It was considered very nutritious!

Glossary

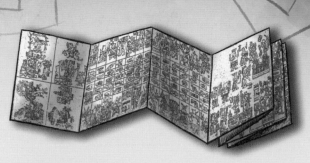

calmecac:
the elite school for those training
to be priests

chinampas:
fields made on artificial islands created
in lakes to grow crops

codex:
the Spanish word for an Aztec book

ixiptla:
a priest chosen to impersonate one of
the gods and then be sacrificed

macehualli
peasants, slaves, and servants

maguey:
a spiky desert plant, like a cactus

patolli:
gambling race game played on a
cross-shaped board

pochteca:
merchants and craftspeople

pulque:
a kind of beer made from the sap of
the maguey plant

quaquacuiltin:
the head priests of the calmecac

tecpan:
a palace or official's home

telpochcalli:
the school for those training to be warriors

teponaztli:
a big drum made from a log

tlachtli:
the ball game played between two teams
who try to knock a heavy rubber ball
through a stone hoop

tlacopotli:
beads that are hung round the neck of a
baby boy destined for the priesthood, to
store his soul until he is ready

tlamacazqui:
a qualified priest or priest of offerings

tlamacazton:
a trainee or little priest

tlenamacac:
a fire priest

volador:
a game in which young men jump from
a high pole with a rope tied around their
waist

yoyotl:
a kind of rattle

INDEX

The Author

John Farndon is Royal Literary Fellow at Anglia Ruskin University in Cambridge, United Kingdom, and the author of a huge number of books for adults and children on science and nature, including international best-sellers. He has been shortlisted four times for the Royal Society's Young People's Book Prize.

The Artist

Giuliano Aloisi graduated from the Institute of Cinema and Television in Rome in 1995, and works an animator and illustrator in advertising and educational publishing. He has contributed to programmes for the Italian TV channel, RAI, and illustrated the comic magazine *Lupo Alberto* (Albert the Wolf, a famous cartoon character in Italy).